MORAL COMPASS: Ethics Recalibrated

(Revisiting Professional Ethics)

Michele Galura Yco

COPYRIGHT © 2022 Moral Compass: Ethics Recalibrated (Revisiting Professional Ethics By Michele Galura Yco

ISBN
Hardbound-978-621-470-360-9
Softbound/Paperback-978-621-470-361-6
MOBI/KINDLE-978-621-470-362-3

Published by:
Poetry Planet Book Publishing House
Rosario, Pozorrubio, Pangasinan,
Philippines
Contact No.: 09554960044
Email: maritesritumalta@gmail.com

PREFACE

Human relations have in integral part in every career success.

The relationships between the employees and the employers or management impacts the kind of culture that may exist in the workplace.

The book capitalizes on reviewing and revisiting concepts on how an individual being part of an organization or an institution develop and maintain a positive work environment.

TABLE OF CONTENTS

PRAYER BEFORE WORK

God, our Loving Father,
We thank you for this wonderful day.
We dearly thank you for the provision of this job.
We commit this workday to you, our dear Lord
and Savior.
Send your Holy Spirit to guide us.
Grant us the gift of wisdom and knowledge as we
start our work today.
Grant us the grace of perseverance and patience
that in everything that we do, we do it for your
greater glory as we continue your mission that we
have inherited, for the salvation of souls.
When we are experiencing worry, help us to
remember that you are in control.
Help us realize that every opportunity is for our
growth in character and skills.
Make us an instrument and source of joy to those
we work with.

Inspire us, so that I may work hard not only for our own benefits but also for the community. We leave every detail of our job situation with you, offering and trusting in your faithfulness. In Jesus' name we ask, Amen.

ETHICS IN THE WORKPLACE

According to Patel (2007), "Human Resource Management is a business function concerned with managing relations between groups of people in their capacity as employees, employers, and managers." This process would mean that some concerns and issues may arise. One of these concerns is work ethics.

As a member of any institution, one must be aware of ethics. One must know and understand the significance of a good work ethic.

Ethics has become more complex, especially in the workplace. The ethical problems encountered may lead to dilemmas and critical circumstances.

Some of the members in the workplace may not be behaving or acting in the way they must be. Ethics is basically concerned with how a moral person should behave. It dictates the course of actions we do in our daily lives. It can be considered the core of the workplace culture. This is what guides us in being truthful and keeping promises. According to the blog (vantage circle) that I have read, and I quote, "work ethics is a set of moral principles or values that an employee abides by and uses in their job performance. It covers an employee's behavior and attitude towards their job, career, and workplace." It is a moral compass. It is the reflection of integrity, honesty, and transparency too.

Even though a lot is aware of what ethics is; still there are some complex issues that may arise — diversity of the people in the workplace, attitude, compliance, professionalism, leadership, workplace culture, conflicts like whistleblowing and rants (even on social media), accountability and the like.

How could all of these be addressed? It is challenging; however, this must be acknowledged. An organization with unresolved ethics issues may result in low productivity, poor morale, and other major concerns. Being in Human Resource Management, everyone must have a thorough understanding of what these issues are. Deter these matters to minimize collisions thus peace and order may be present in the workplace.

Good Work Ethics

How could we determine if the members of an organization practice good work ethics in the workplace? Are you aware of them? Do you practice them?

Let me present to you a list of how one could manifest good work ethics in the workplace. Mark √ all that applies to you.

Punctuality

___I am punctual because most of the time I arrived 10 to 30 minutes earlier in the workplace, meetings, conventions, or seminars.

___I keep records of what must be accomplished (to-do list, calendar of activities, timetable)

___I do care about meeting deadlines. I avoid being the cause of delay.

___I do not absent from work or make unnecessary excuses to avoid responsibilities.

___I respect my colleagues. As much as possible, I manage to avoid tardiness.

Being punctual means that you do care about everyone - your team, your management, or the organization's welfare.

Professionalism

___I show and maintain effective working relationships and habits with my colleagues.

___I process the root cause of problems - As much as possible, I see to it that I am part of the solution, and not the problem.

___I demonstrate integrity, honesty, transparency, and trustworthiness.

___I develop self-awareness most of the time. I make sure that I manage my emotions so that I won't trigger any negative feelings toward others and my work.

___I project professional presence at all times like dressing appropriately (rule of the thumb).

Professionalism - "The skill, good judgment, and polite behavior that is expected from a person who is trained to do a job well" Merriam-Webster, n.d.t

Desire to improve

___I do care about personal and professional development. I look forward to opportunities that may help me be a better version of myself.

___I take smart feedback positively.

___I set goals and action plans to address lapses and missed expectations.

___I sign up for training, seminars, and learning action cells (local and international),

___I am open to wearing multiple hats not to impress but to check my abilities and limitations.

The desire to improve means one is willing to make positive changes for the better - bringing out the best version of oneself.

Good Example

____ I set a good influence on others in the workplace.

____ I never promote gossiping in the workplace.

____ I encourage others to manifest good behavior with positive illustrations or actions. Just like responding accordingly to good-natured jokes.

____ I walk the talk.

____ I lead by example.

Do what you preach. It is necessary to act accordingly and appropriately in the workplace all the time.

Responsibility and Accountability

____I turn up work on time and see to it that I accomplish tasks given completely.

____I admit mistakes and I take responsibility for my actions.

____I accept responsibility and make sure that I employ teamwork to achieve the set goals.

____I do what my job description states and I adhere to the policies of my organization or institution.

___I do my best to successfully execute my job responsibilities.

Responsibility and accountability go hand in hand. They reciprocate each other. Your responsibility is to be responsibly accountable for all your words, actions, and deeds.

Attitude

___I show respect to my employers, managers, colleagues, and clients.

___I project commitment to my job.

___I initiate assistance to others if there is a need to.

___I share ideas that might be of great help to others and offer support to improve productivity in the workplace.

___I commit to positivity to maintain a peaceful and conducive work environment.

How we deal with ourselves and with others in the workplace reflects one's attitude. It impacts everyone in the workplace. We must be very careful and mindful about our attitude towards work and towards our colleagues.

References:

Defining Professionalism. Retrieved https://www.queensu.ca/teachingandlearning/modules/ethics/11_s3_03_defining_professionalism.html

Patel, Sonakshi. 2007. Ethics and Human Resource Management Chapter outline. Retrieved shorturl.at/bkPTW

Paycor. 2020. 7 Characteristics of a Good Work Ethic. Retrieved https://www.paycor.com/resource-center/articles/7-characteristics-of-a-good-work-ethic/

SpriggHR. 2020. 6 Ethical Issues in Business and What to Do About Them. Retrieved https://sprigghr.com/blog/hr-professionals/6-ethical-issues-in-business-and-what-to-do-about-them/

Vintage Circle. 2022. 10 Ways To Develop Strong Work Ethics Among Employees. Retrieved https://blog.vantagecircle.com/work-ethics/

Virginia Tech. 2022. Career and Professional Development. Professionalism. Retrieved https://career.vt.edu/develop/professionalism.html

Belcher, Lynda Moultry. 2019. Chron. Five Attitudes That Are Important in Workplaces. Retrieved https://smallbusiness.chron.com/five-attitudes-important-workplaces-19114.html

I, AS A COLLEAGUE...

How do we contribute to the betterment of the workplace culture? Who am I as a colleague to others in our organization? These are some of the testimonies or messages from my colleagues.

I will show my respect to others and do my responsibilities with utmost diligence and enthusiasm.

-*Ma'am Krisma*

I will help others in any way I can, to achieve the institution's vision with happiness.

-

Cheecy

I will be a good team player and will work hand in hand with my colleagues.

(SFE)

I will work to the best of my ability, treat my colleagues with respect, and have a positive attitude to inspire, influence and empower my team. Just like Vala Asfar said, we are not a team because we work together. We are a team because we respect, trust and care for each other.

GLP

I will do my best with my ability and capability to work hand in hand with my colleagues."

(DRS)

"I will foster a sense of camaraderie and treat everyone with utmost respect.

(RBL)

I will always see the good things in everyone.

(MPF)

I will selflessly share my knowledge and skills to my constituents to deliver quality services.

-BURN

I will strengthen communication with them because it helps in building a harmonious relationship and that it could promote teamwork.

- BLL

I will be a C-A-T :) Confidant-someone they could turn to; Afflatus-someone who would be an inspiration; and Trustworthy-someone who is truthful and honest about my job, my employers, and my colleagues.

- CER

MORAL COMPASS

Moral compass points in the right direction

Opens the mind and heart to know what is right and wrong

Reminds us to be mindful of our words, thoughts, and actions at all times

Act accordingly is the tagline that would best suit it

Limits people from being judgmental, greedy, and self-centered individuals

Consequences go through when (moral compass) is compromised

Observes and makes ethical decisions - may lessen the possibility of conflict and harm to others

Moral purpose values employee's inner being, acknowledging their worth

Promotes staying true to one's values

Acknowledges one's moral code that is consistently aware of what is right and wrong

Synchronizes mindset with actions and words

Seeks to know the truth, practices fairness, creates and builds goodwill and friendship, and determines all that is beneficial to everyone.

Reference:

Moral Compass: What Is It and How to Use It.
2021. Retrieved October 17, 2022
https://ofhsoupkitchen.org/moral-compass

Professional Development as an Investment

"Education is the most powerful weapon which
you can use to change the world."
– Nelson Mandela

Professional development is used in reference to a wide variety of specialized career training, formal education, or advanced professional learning intended to help individuals improve their professional knowledge, competence, skill, and stay up-to-date on current trends. While it is true that education is a never-ending process, a person can continue to earn a degree and start a career. Through continuing education, career-minded individuals can constantly improve their skills and become more proficient at their jobs

Why Professional Development?

- **Professional development includes enhancing oneself in understanding the type of job to which an individual needs to improve**. It entails improving the necessary skills to perform one's role effectively for it is something that will continue throughout the working life.

- ***Professional development ensures knowledge and understanding the area of expertise for the acquisition of career advancemen**t*. Gaining professional development is indeed helpful for those who want to hone and explore more of their abilities.

- *Professional development opens opportunities and doors for future career changes*. Employees will become better workers through professional development. Learning the right skills for their career, employees will be more productive and efficient in their work.

In order to achieve success in one's career, it requires ongoing training and education where professional development comes in. Professional development is more than just training, it prepares an individual to make new contributions in the workplace.

QUOTES AT WORK!

"Claim fruitful days ahead."

"Failure is one of the integral events in life, it is part of success."

"Sometimes we have to look for a new angle to visualize what's good is coming."

"Saying no is not a form of weakness, it is valuing and loving ourselves."

"Appreciate your small wins."

"Be a pusher of excellence, compassion, and empathy."

"Start from within and everything resonates."

"Our actions will speak for our thoughts and feelings."

"Greater things are coming—just wait patiently."

"Share what you can, give what you can, and show what is exemplary emulating."

"Whatever rewards and recognitions you receive, stay rooted on the ground."

"Do not engage in something you are not passionate about."

"Struggles at work will be the foundation of that leader in you."

"

Worthy

"Let your light shine in front of men. Then they will see the good things you do and will honor your Father who is in heaven."

(Matthew 5:16)

Open-minded

"You who are servants who are owned by someone, obey your owners. Work hard for them all the time, not just when they are watching you. Work for them as you would for the Lord because you honor God."

(Colossians 3:22)

Resilience

"You shall eat the fruit of the labor of your hands; you shall be blessed, and it shall be well with you."

(Psalm 128:2)

Kind-hearted

"Commit your work to the Lord, and your plans will be established."

(Proverbs 16:3)

WORKPLACE CULTURE – IT'S DEFINITION AND IMPORTANCE

An employee went home happily after a tedious day at work. His wife asked him how he can manage to feel overwhelmed and enthusiastic despite his tiresome day. The husband responded positively – "I feel satisfied and happy at work. I am valued with all my contributions. We have a productive environment."

The scenario above makes it obvious what workplace culture is about. According to Forbes, workplace culture is "the environment that surrounds us all the time." It is also a "collection of attitudes, beliefs and behaviors that make up the regular atmosphere in a work environment," says the jobs website Indeed.

So, how do you describe your company's or institution's workplace culture?

Let us discuss some important matters about it. These are some of the questions we will answer. Are you ready?

Do you think workplace culture is significant? Why?

What impacts workplace culture?

Can we create a positive workplace culture?

WORKPLACE CULTURE IS SIGNIFICANT – WHY?

Imagine an institution without a culture. This would mean no shared values, no belief system, no individual upbringing, teamwork is impossible, and productivity is devastatingly low.

Work culture is important for the reason that it elevates the morale of every individual. There is a positive mindset which could lead to a growth mentality.

Since work culture speaks about the attitudes and behaviors of employees within an organization, it is indeed important to take into consideration how to keep the employees' good, caring, adaptive, cooperative, and resilient attitudes and behaviors.

This pictures how every individual in an institution may affect one another through their actions, words, values, and work manners. These will cultivate the kind of environment that will evolve within the organization.

Workplace culture is important because:

- ✓ It keeps talented staff – they enjoy what they do.
- ✓ It keeps employees engaged in their work.
- ✓ It promotes healthy communication and openness,

encouraging employees to voice what they feel and think.
✓ It makes all employees feel satisfaction at work thus increasing their productivity.
✓ It makes success feasible = happy employees + positive workplace culture.

WHAT IMPACTS WORKPLACE CULTURE?

Scenario A

As I stepped up the stairs of the company that I am applying to, I could say that it is a decent one. Upon entrance, I could clearly see the directory. There is an information desk with an attendant who is well-dressed, attentive, and polite. The place is not air-conditioned but with enough electric fans (wall fans and stand fans), I don't bother the hot weather of the day. It is well-ventilated.

While I am waiting for my turn to be called, I was instructed to sit in the waiting area. I could tell how the other applicants sit comfortably while they sip cold water and hot coffee. Yes! There is a water dispenser available for everyone. Though it's not free, at least it is a comfort drink for all. It seems that the workplace has a conducive and positive vibe because the employees are warm and welcoming.

Scenario B

It is a typical day for an applicant like me. I am excited to see my future workplace. As I stepped into the hallway, it is evident that it is a busy place to be. The information desk attendant is hectic on her phone and impolitely frowns as people come by for inquiries. It seems that she is having a bad day. The place is fully air-conditioned however, you could feel the uneasiness of the people around due to lack of chairs in the waiting area.

Upon observation, some of the employees seemed to ignore each other. They seldom smile and are overwhelmed with work. I could feel how tough work is here.

What can you say?

The company leaders set the company's culture through their rules or policies, benefits, goals, vision, and mission.

How the leaders shape and mold the kind of culture they want in their company depends on their selection of applicants too. The physical environment of a workplace could influence the company's culture as well.

It is equally important to consider that all companies and organizations, no matter how big or small the business is – must invest in its:

- Physical environment (includes chairs, cubicles, tables, comfort rooms, ventilation, space, and the like)
- Lightings
- Perks (if possible)
- Amenities (if possible, like gyms or break rooms)

The physical environment of a workplace impacts the mood, tone, and vibe of its employees. These serve as healthy determinants which contribute to the well-being of the people in it.

CAN WE CREATE A POSITIVE WORKPLACE CULTURE?

Are you familiar with these lines?

Oh, my goodness, this place is toxic and so are the people!

I want an early retirement. The work is exhausting. The environment is no longer healthy.

How can I survive in this kind of work culture?

I don't feel important. I don't think they still want me here.

How could they not see how hard I've worked?

I feel stagnant. There is no personal and professional growth here.

It's another day for overtime.

Workplace culture is also about how one acts in the workplace. How could leaders make the best out of their employees?

Appreciate employees through awards and recognitions. When employees work and perform beyond their limits and expectations, it is proper to credit and acknowledge their hard work. This kind of act boosts employees and will motivate them to work better in the future.

Develop employees to navigate career challenges. According to Jennifer Herrity, a career coach at Indeed, employees must stay motivated and skilled. Developing them gives rise to a more driven workforce. This directly impacts and affects the institution or company's performance.

Give regular feedback. Giving constructive and helpful feedback to employees help them become more productive and this will encourage them to improve and be better always.

Appoint responsibilities. If employees are given higher or special responsibilities and tasks to undertake, these uplift their morale and boost their self-esteem. This means that employers believe and trust the capabilities of their employees.

Involve coaching and mentoring. Coaching and mentoring employees help them to see things innovatively. A new perspective and learning may lead to a valuable and productive employee.

Take career advancement seriously. Every employee wants a promotion and is looking forward to a greener pasture at their endeavor. Employees don't want to feel stagnant. They might be demotivated if career progression is not taken importance. They would want to look for better opportunities outside the organization.

An employee who is valued and respected for all his rights will always aim to work with love, effort, dedication, and passion. Recognizing their skills, talents, contributions, and successes will eventually inspire them to keep going. Sharing a positive spirit within the workplace makes it lighter to work amidst tons of goals to fulfill and other hassles and deadlines.

References:

What is workplace culture? Retrieved October 9, 2021. https://www.workplace.com/blog/workplace-culture

Indeed Editorial Team. March 31, 2020. What Is Work Culture? Retrieved October 9, 2021. https://www.indeed.com/career-advice/career-development/work-culture

Factorial HR. July 20, 2022. Work Culture Definition: What Does It Really Mean? Retrieved October 9, 2021. https://factorialhr.com/blog/work-culture-definition/#important

Trends, Data & Insights. June 30, 2022. What Is Workplace Culture Really? Retrieved October 9, 2021. https://sidekicker.com/au/blog/workplace-culture-really/

Create a Positive Workplace Culture For Your Employees. March 13, 2022. Retrieved October 16, 2022. https://engagedly.com/creating-a-positive-workplace-culture/#:~:text=Recognize%20And%20Reward%20Good%20Work&text=So%2C%20when%20employees%20perform%20beyond,perform%20better%20in%20the%20future.

Herrity, Jennifer. 2021. 14 Effective Tips for Developing Employees. Retrieved October 16, 2022. https://www.indeed.com/career-advice/career-development/developing-employee.

YOUR ATTITUDE MATTERS IN THE WORKPLACE

Everyone has a different attitude when it comes to work. Attitude is something that influences the ability of an individual to move or respond in every aspect of life. Here are some of the things that we need to remember on the importance of acknowledging our attitude:

- ***It determines an individual's perception.***
  Our attitude gives us direct insight into our thoughts, emotions, and beliefs.Workers with a positive attitude toward work are more likely passionate and committed in their quest for success. They feel motivated to learn new things.

- ***It is a personal choice.***
  Our attitude determines how we react to adversity and challenges. Constant reminder to our self that success entails sacrifice. It cannot be attained in just a snap of a finger. As Winston Churchill once said, **" Attitude is a little thing**

that makes a big difference. " Consider many possibilities before making a decision. It will help us get the results and outcomes that we hope for in the future.

- ***It builds character.***

  Our attitude enables us to learn how to establish better rapport with our co - workers. We need to feel motivated to learn new things and share your skills in the workplace. All the members are united and work for a common cause. Your positive attitude enables you to work as a team as you move up in achieving common objectives . Steve Jobs claimed that. ***"The only way to do great work is to love what you do."*** Love what you do in the workplace not only because it is required or stated in your job description, instead it gives you self fulfillment.

ABOUT THE AUTHOR

MICHELE GALURA YCO is a committed and passionate public servant of the Department of Education since2003. She is a true reflection of integrity in her field as an Administrative Officer in her current station, San Matias National High School located in Sto. Tomas, Pampanga. She is not only a hard-working employee but also a public-spirited co-worker.

As a graduate of Master Degree in Public Administration at Don Honorio Ventura State University, Bacolor, Pampanga gives substance to her quest for continuous professional growth that lead her to try writing her first book.

Behind the unnumbered nights of conceptualizing the content of her first book is the noblest goal of sharing her actual experiences to serve as an inspiration not only to fellow government workers but also other people who are already in the same line of field or planning to be one. She believes that her first book could be a significant instrument in the development of holistic character of employees.

This unique author is a native of Mexico, Pampanga. She is a wife and a mother of two children. And surely after reading her book, you will likely crave for more of her succeeding writings.